"SALES SYMPHONY"

Harmonizing Strategies for success in the Evolving Business Landscape

Author: Saurabh Kumar

CONTENTS

INTRODUCTION:

Welcome to "Sales Symphony" a comprehensive guide designed to equip you with the skills and strategies necessary to excel in the dynamic world of sales. Whether you are a seasoned sales professional looking to refine your techniques or a beginner eager to navigate the intricacies of the sales landscape, this ebook is tailored to meet your needs.

PREFACE

Welcome to the world of sales excellence! In an era where business landscapes evolve rapidly, mastering the art and science of sales is a journey filled with challenges, triumphs, and endless opportunities for growth. This comprehensive guide is designed to be your trusted companion on this exciting expedition, providing insights and strategies that span the spectrum of sales—from foundational principles to advanced techniques, and from relationship-building to fostering innovation.

In the pages that follow, you will embark on a transformative exploration of the sales domain. Whether you are a seasoned professional seeking to refine your approach or a budding entrepreneur eager to grasp the essentials, this guide aims to cater to a diverse audience. It is our belief that sales is not merely a transactional process; it is a dynamic and intricate dance between individuals, organizations, and the ever-changing market forces.

This guide unfolds in eight chapters, each dedicated to a critical aspect of sales excellence. We begin by laying the groundwork, understanding the fundamentals, and building a strong foundation. As we progress, we delve into the art of effective communication, advanced closing strategies, and the intricacies of customer relationship management.

Adaptability is a cornerstone of sales success, and hence, we explore strategies for navigating changing markets and industry trends. The journey concludes by spotlighting the importance of sustaining excellence through continuous innovation and forward-thinking approaches.

We encourage you not only to read this guide but to engage with its content actively. Apply the principles discussed, reflect on your experiences, and embrace the iterative nature of learning in the sales domain. Each chapter is crafted to be a practical and actionable resource, providing you with the tools to navigate the complex terrain of modern sales.

The world of sales is dynamic, challenging, and incredibly rewarding. As you embark on this enlightening journey, may this guide be a source of inspiration, guidance, and empowerment. Here's to unlocking your full potential in sales and achieving excellence in every interaction.

Best wishes on your sales journey,

Saurabh Kumar
Sales Consultant
saurabhapr30@gmail.com

CHAPTER 1: UNDERSTANDING THE FUNDAMENTALS OF SALES

Sales, often regarded as the lifeblood of any business, is a multifaceted discipline that goes beyond the simple act of exchanging goods or services for money. In this chapter, we delve into the core principles that form the foundation of successful salesmanship.

1.1 Definition and Importance of Sales

Sales, in its essence, is the process of persuading and influencing potential customers to make a purchase. It involves a strategic and dynamic interaction between a seller and a buyer, with the ultimate goal of satisfying the needs and wants of the customer while achieving the objectives of the seller.

Understanding the importance of sales is crucial for any individual or organization aiming for sustained growth. Effective sales drive revenue, create brand awareness, and foster long-term relationships with customers. Whether you are a solo entrepreneur, a sales professional, or part of a large corporation, a solid grasp of the significance of sales is fundamental to achieving success in the competitive business landscape.

1.2 The Sales Process: A Step-by-Step Overview

The sales process is a structured series of steps that guide a potential customer from initial awareness to making a purchase. While the specific steps may vary depending on the industry and product, a typical sales process includes:

1.2.1 Prospecting:
Identifying and qualifying potential leads who may be interested in your product or service.

1.2.2 Initial Contact:
Reaching out to potential customers to introduce your offering and build a connection.

1.2.3 Needs Assessment:
Understanding the customer's needs, challenges, and desires to tailor your pitch effectively.

1.2.4 Presentation:
Showcasing your product or service in a compelling manner, addressing the customer's pain points.

1.2.5 Handling Objections:
Addressing concerns or hesitations the customer may have to move them closer to a decision.

1.2.6 Closing the Sale:
Securing the commitment to purchase through effective closing techniques.

1.2.7 Follow-up:
Maintaining post-sale communication to ensure customer satisfaction and encourage loyalty.

1.2 Types of Sales: B2B vs. B2C

Sales can be broadly categorized into Business-to-Business (B2B) and Business-to-Consumer (B2C). Understanding the nuances of each type is crucial for tailoring your approach:

1.3.1 B2B Sales:
Focused on selling products or services to other businesses. Involves longer sales cycles, relationship-building, and a thorough understanding of the business needs of the client.

1.3.2 B2C Sales:
Targeted at individual consumers. Often characterized by shorter sales cycles, emotional appeals, and a focus on mass marketing.

1.4 The Role of Emotional Intelligence in Sales

Emotional Intelligence (EI) plays a pivotal role in sales success. The ability to understand and manage one's own emotions while empathetically connecting with the emotions of others can significantly impact the sales process. In this section, we explore how emotional intelligence influences:

1.4.1 Building Rapport:

Establishing a genuine connection with customers by understanding their emotions and motivations.

1.4.2 Active Listening:

Empathetic listening to comprehend customer needs and concerns.

1.4.3 Handling Rejections:

Maintaining composure and resilience in the face of rejection or objections.

1.4.4 Building Long-Term Relationships:

Fostering trust and loyalty through emotional intelligence for sustained customer relationships.

1.4.5 Conflict Resolution:

Effectively navigating conflicts and disputes, turning challenges into opportunities for stronger relationships.

1.4.6 Adapting to Customer Personalities:

Recognizing and adapting to diverse personalities and communication styles for more successful interactions.

1.4.7 Empathy in Customer Service:

Understanding the customer's perspective and demonstrating empathy to enhance the overall customer experience.

Emotional intelligence is not just a soft skill; it's a powerful tool that can differentiate a good salesperson from a great one. As you cultivate emotional intelligence in your sales approach, you'll find yourself better equipped to navigate the complexities of human interactions, leading to increased trust, improved communication, and ultimately, higher sales success rates.

Applying the Fundamentals in Real-world Scenarios

To reinforce the concepts discussed in this chapter, consider real-world scenarios that illustrate the application of sales fundamentals:

Scenario 1: B2B Consultative Selling

Imagine you're a sales representative for a software company targeting other businesses. Applying the B2B sales model, your focus is on understanding the unique needs and challenges of each client. By conducting thorough needs assessments and tailoring your presentations to showcase how your software addresses specific business pain points, you build trust and credibility, key components in successful B2B relationships.

Scenario 2: B2C Emotional Selling

Now, picture yourself in a B2C setting, selling high-end fashion accessories directly to consumers. Here, emotional intelligence comes into play as you connect with customers on a personal level. Understanding their emotions, desires, and preferences allows you to make emotionally resonant pitches, creating a memorable and positive buying experience that goes beyond the product itself.

Scenario 3: Handling Customer Objections with Emotional Intelligence

In any sales scenario, objections are inevitable. Consider a situation where a potential customer raises concerns about the pricing of your product. Instead of responding defensively, an emotionally intelligent salesperson would acknowledge the customer's concerns, express understanding, and pivot the conversation to highlight the value and benefits of the product. This empathetic approach can turn objections into opportunities to reinforce the product's worth.

"Understanding these fundamental aspects of sales sets the stage for the in-depth exploration of advanced strategies and techniques in the subsequent chapters. As you proceed in your sales journey, remember that mastering the basics is key to achieving excellence in the dynamic field of sales."

"As you progress through this ebook, remember that the fundamentals discussed in this chapter serve as the bedrock for advanced sales strategies. Whether you're engaging in B2B or B2C sales, the principles of effective communication, understanding customer needs, and leveraging emotional intelligence will remain integral to your success. The subsequent chapters will be built upon these fundamentals, providing you with a comprehensive toolkit for mastering the art of sales."

CHAPTER 2: BUILDING A STRONG SALES FOUNDATION

In the realm of sales, success is not merely a product of tactics and strategies; it begins with a solid foundation rooted in the right mindset, clear goals, product knowledge, and a deep understanding of your target audience. This chapter explores the essential elements that constitute a strong sales foundation.

2.1 Developing a Sales Mindset

Your mindset is the lens through which you view your role in sales. Developing a positive and growth-oriented sales mindset is paramount to your success. Consider the following aspects:

2.1.1 Embrace a Positive Attitude:

Maintaining a positive attitude, even in the face of challenges, allows you to approach each interaction with enthusiasm and resilience.

2.1.2 Continuous Learning:

Adopt a mindset of continuous learning. The sales landscape evolves, and staying updated on industry trends, customer behaviors, and new technologies will keep you ahead of the curve.

2.1.3 Resilience in the Face of Rejection:

Understand that rejection is a natural part of sales. A resilient mindset enables you to bounce back from setbacks, learn from experiences, and refine your approach.

2.1.4 Customer-Centric Focus:

Shift your focus from selling products to solving customer problems. A customer-centric mindset builds trust and establishes long-term relationships.

2.2 Setting SMART Sales Goals

Goals provide direction and purpose in sales. Using the SMART (Specific, Measurable, Achievable, Relevant, Time-bound) framework ensures that your goals are clear, realistic, and conducive to success:

2.2.1 Specific:

Define specific sales objectives, such as increasing revenue, acquiring new clients, or expanding market share.

2.2.2 Measurable:

Quantify your goals to track progress. For example, set a target percentage increase in sales or a specific number of new customers.

2.2.3 Achievable:

Set goals that are challenging but attainable. Consider your current resources, market conditions, and capabilities.

2.2.4 Relevant:

Align your sales goals with broader business objectives. Ensure they contribute to the overall success and growth of the organization.

2.2.5 Time-bound:

Establish a timeline for achieving your sales goals. This adds a sense of urgency and helps in prioritizing tasks.

2.3 Know Your Product Inside Out

Product knowledge is the cornerstone of effective selling. To convincingly communicate the value of your offering, you must:

2.3.1 Understand Features and Benefits:
Articulate not only the features of your product but also how these features directly benefit the customer.

2.3.2 Anticipate Customer Questions:
Being well-versed in your product allows you to anticipate and address potential customer questions or concerns proactively.

2.3.3 Stay Updated on Product Changes:
Products evolve, and it's crucial to stay informed about updates, enhancements, or new features. This ensures accurate and up-to-date information when interacting with customers.

2.3.4 Relate Features to Customer Needs:
Link product features to specific customer needs. This connection demonstrates how your product is a solution to their challenges.

2.4 Identifying Your Target Audience

Understanding your target audience is fundamental to tailoring your sales approach. Consider the following steps:

2.4.1 Market Research:
Conduct thorough market research to identify your ideal customer profile. Analyze demographics, behaviors, and preferences.

2.4.2 Create Buyer Personas:
Develop detailed buyer personas representing different segments of your target audience. This helps in crafting personalized and

effective sales messages.

2.4.3 Segment Your Audience:

Recognize that your audience may have diverse needs. Segmenting your target audience allows for more targeted and impactful sales strategies.

2.4.4 Stay Customer-Centric:

Place the customer at the center of your sales efforts. Understanding their pain points and desires enables you to tailor your approach for maximum impact.

By cultivating a sales mindset, setting SMART goals, mastering product knowledge, and understanding your target audience, you lay the groundwork for success in the competitive world of sales. As you progress through this ebook, remember that a strong foundation is the springboard to advanced sales strategies and sustained excellence in your sales endeavors.

Applying the Foundation in Practice

To reinforce the importance of building a strong sales foundation, let's consider how a sales professional might apply these principles in real-world scenarios:

Scenario 1: Developing a Sales Mindset

Imagine you are a sales representative for a start-up entering a competitive market. Instead of being discouraged by the challenges, you embrace a positive attitude. You view each rejection as an opportunity to learn and adjust your approach. This mindset not only keeps you motivated but also allows you to maintain enthusiasm and resilience, essential qualities in the face of uncertainty.

Scenario 2: Setting SMART Sales Goals

As a sales manager, you set SMART goals for your team to increase quarterly sales revenue. The goals are specific, focusing on acquiring new clients and upselling to existing ones. They are measurable, with clear metrics to track progress. Achievability is considered by aligning goals with the team's skills and resources. The relevance of the goals is evident in their contribution to the overall growth strategy, and a time-bound approach adds urgency to the team's efforts.

Scenario 3: Knowing Your Product Inside Out

In a customer meeting, your in-depth knowledge of the product allows you to highlight its unique features and benefits. You anticipate and address questions with ease, demonstrating a thorough understanding of how the product addresses the specific needs of the customer. Your confidence and product expertise instill trust and credibility, making the customer more receptive to your pitch.

Scenario 4: Identifying Your Target Audience

Suppose you are launching a new line of fitness products. Through extensive market research, you identify your target audience as health-conscious individuals aged 25-40 with an interest in at-home workouts. Creating detailed buyer personas helps tailor marketing messages and sales pitches to resonate with this audience. By understanding their preferences and pain points, you can position your products as the ideal solution for their fitness needs.

Continuous Improvement and Adaptation

Building a strong sales foundation is not a one-time effort but an ongoing process. Regularly revisit and reassess your mindset, goals, product knowledge, and understanding of your target audience. Stay attuned to industry trends, customer feedback, and market changes. Adaptability and a commitment to continuous improvement will ensure that your sales foundation remains robust and resilient in the ever-evolving business landscape.

In the upcoming chapters, we will delve into more advanced sales strategies and techniques, building upon the solid foundation established here. As you progress in your sales journey, remember that **success is not just about closing deals; it's about creating lasting value for your customers and contributing to the overall growth and success of your organization.**

CHAPTER 3: EFFECTIVE COMMUNICATION IN SALES

Communication is the lifeblood of successful sales interactions. In this chapter, we explore the intricacies of effective communication, encompassing active listening, compelling sales pitches, objection handling, and the development of strong rapport with customers.

3.1 The Power of Active Listening

Active listening is a fundamental skill that sets the stage for meaningful communication. By fully engaging with your customers, you gain valuable insights into their needs and concerns. Key components of active listening include:

3.1.1 Empathetic Understanding:
Putting yourself in the customer's shoes and genuinely comprehending their perspective fosters trust and strengthens the customer-salesperson relationship.

3.1.2 Clarification and Confirmation:
Seeking clarification on customer statements and confirming your understanding demonstrates your commitment to accurately addressing their needs.

3.1.3 Non-Verbal Cues:

Paying attention to non-verbal cues such as body language and facial expressions enhances your ability to interpret and respond effectively to customer emotions.

3.1.4 Patience:

Allowing customers to express themselves fully without interruption demonstrates respect and patience, contributing to a positive customer experience.

Additional Insights:

Ask Open-Ended Questions: Encourage customers to share more by asking open-ended questions. This not only provides valuable information but also demonstrates your genuine interest in understanding their needs.

Practical Tips:

Paraphrasing: Repeat or paraphrase what the customer has said to ensure mutual understanding. This shows that you are actively engaged and committed to accurate communication.

3.2 Crafting a Compelling Sales Pitch

A well-crafted sales pitch is a powerful tool for capturing customer attention and driving engagement. The elements of an effective sales pitch include:

3.2.1 Understanding Customer Pain Points:

Tailoring your pitch to address specific customer challenges demonstrates that you've invested time in understanding their needs.

3.2.2 Clear Value Proposition:

Clearly articulating the unique value your product or service offers helps customers understand how it meets their requirements better than alternatives.

3.2.3 Storytelling:
Weaving a narrative that resonates with the customer emotionally can create a memorable and persuasive impact, making your pitch more compelling.

3.2.4 Customization:
Adapting your pitch to align with the customer's preferences, communication style, and interests enhances its relevance and effectiveness.

Additional Insights:

Focus on Benefits, Not Just Features: While it's crucial to highlight product features, center your pitch around how these features directly benefit the customer. This customer-centric approach makes your pitch more compelling.

Practical Tips:

Tailor Pitches to Different Audiences: Customize your pitch based on the audience. Executives may be interested in cost savings, while end-users may be more concerned with usability. Adapt your message accordingly.

3.3 Overcoming Objections

Objections are a natural part of the sales process and should be viewed as opportunities to provide additional information and address concerns. Key strategies for overcoming objections include:

3.3.1 Anticipating Common Objections:
Being proactive by addressing potential objections before they arise showcases your expertise and minimizes customer hesitations.

3.3.2 Empathetic Response:

Responding to objections with empathy and understanding reassures the customer that their concerns are acknowledged and taken seriously.

3.3.3 Providing Solutions:

Rather than dismissing objections, focus on presenting viable solutions that showcase the value and benefits of your product or service.

3.3.4 Handling Price Objections:

Effectively communicating the value proposition and emphasizing the return on investment helps mitigate concerns related to pricing.

Additional Insights:

Anticipate and Address Objections Proactively: Before objections arise, anticipate potential concerns and address them in your presentation. This proactive approach showcases your expertise and builds confidence.

Practical Tips:

Use Success Stories: Share success stories or case studies where similar objections were overcome, demonstrating real-world examples of how your product or service has provided value.

3.4 Building Rapport with Customers

Building strong rapport is the foundation of a lasting customer relationship. Techniques for fostering rapport include:

3.4.1 Authenticity:

Being genuine and authentic in your interactions establishes trust and credibility with customers.

3.4.2 Finding Common Ground:

Identifying shared interests or experiences helps create a connection beyond the transactional aspect of the sales relationship.

3.4.3 Consistent Communication:

Maintaining regular and transparent communication builds confidence and reinforces the customer's trust in your reliability.

3.4.4 Post-Sale Relationship Building:

Continuing to nurture the relationship after the sale through follow-up and ongoing support enhances customer satisfaction and loyalty.

Additional Insights:

Adapt Communication Style: Pay attention to the customer's communication style and adapt accordingly. Some customers prefer detailed information, while others appreciate a more concise and to-the-point approach.

Practical Tips:

Find Common Ground: Establishing common ground helps build a connection. Whether it's shared interests, experiences, or industry knowledge, finding commonality fosters rapport.

Additional General Insights for Effective Communication in Sales

Emotional Resonance: Connect with customers on an emotional level. Emotions often play a significant role in decision-making, and an emotionally resonant message can leave a lasting impression.

Clear and Concise Messaging: Avoid jargon and overly complex language. Clearly communicate the value proposition using language that resonates with the customer's understanding.

Feedback Loop: Encourage customers to provide feedback during the sales process. This two-way communication fosters collaboration, helps address concerns in real-time, and shows your commitment to customer satisfaction.

Adaptability: Be flexible in your communication style. Different customers may respond better to various approaches, so being adaptable ensures effective communication in diverse situations.

By incorporating these additional insights and practical tips, you can further refine your communication skills in sales. Remember that effective communication is a dynamic and evolving skill that can be continuously honed to meet the unique needs of your customers and the ever-changing business landscape.

In the subsequent chapters, we will delve into the integration of technology in sales, exploring the use of Customer Relationship Management (CRM) systems, social media strategies, and email marketing to enhance communication and streamline the sales process. As you apply the principles of effective communication in your sales endeavors, remember that building genuine connections is the cornerstone of successful and enduring customer relationships.

CHAPTER 4: LEVERAGING TECHNOLOGY IN SALES

In today's digitally driven landscape, the effective use of technology can significantly enhance sales efficiency and effectiveness. This chapter explores the integration of technology into sales processes, covering Customer Relationship Management (CRM) systems, social media strategies, email marketing, and the use of data analytics.

4.1 CRM Systems: Streamlining Your Sales Process

Customer Relationship Management (CRM) systems are invaluable tools for organizing, automating, and synchronizing sales activities. Key aspects of leveraging CRM systems include:

4.1.1 Centralized Customer Data:

Maintaining a centralized repository of customer information allows for a holistic view of interactions, facilitating personalized and targeted communication.

4.1.2 Sales Pipeline Management:

Using CRM to track and manage the sales pipeline enables sales teams to prioritize leads, forecast sales, and identify areas for improvement.

4.1.3 Automation of Routine Tasks:

Automating repetitive tasks such as data entry, email follow-ups, and appointment scheduling frees up valuable time for sales professionals to focus on high-impact activities.

4.1.4 Integration with Other Tools:

Ensuring seamless integration with other tools and platforms enhances the overall efficiency of the sales process, from lead generation to closing deals.

4.2 Social Media and Sales

Social media platforms offer a dynamic space for engaging with prospects and customers. Effectively leveraging social media in sales involves:

4.2.1 Building an Online Presence:

Establishing a strong and professional presence on social media platforms enhances brand visibility and credibility.

4.2.2 Targeted Social Selling:

Identifying and connecting with potential customers on social media allows for more personalized and direct engagement.

4.2.3 Content Sharing and Thought Leadership:

Sharing relevant and valuable content positions you as an industry expert, fostering trust and attracting a loyal audience.

4.2.4 Social Listening:

Monitoring social media channels for mentions, comments, and industry trends provides valuable insights that can inform your sales strategy.

4.3 Email Marketing Strategies

Email remains a powerful tool in the sales arsenal when used strategically. Key components of effective email marketing in sales include:

4.3.1 Segmentation:
Segmenting your email lists based on customer characteristics allows for targeted and personalized communication.

4.3.2 Compelling Content:
Crafting engaging and relevant email content, such as newsletters, product updates, and exclusive offers, keeps your audience informed and interested.

4.3.3 Automation:
Implementing email automation streamlines communication, ensuring timely follow-ups and personalized responses without manual effort.

4.3.4 Analytics and Optimization:
Analyzing email campaign performance provides insights into what resonates with your audience, enabling continuous optimization for better results.

4.4 Using Data Analytics to Enhance Sales Performance

Data analytics empowers sales teams with actionable insights for informed decision-making. Key aspects of leveraging data analytics in sales include:

4.4.1 Predictive Analytics:
Utilizing predictive analytics helps forecast sales trends, identify potential leads, and optimize resource allocation.

4.4.2 Customer Segmentation:
Segmenting customers based on behavior, preferences, and demographics allows for targeted and personalized sales

strategies.

4.4.3 Sales Performance Metrics:
Tracking key performance indicators (KPIs) provides a quantitative measure of sales effectiveness, facilitating continuous improvement.

4.4.4 Data-Driven Decision Making:
Making informed decisions based on data analysis ensures a strategic and adaptive approach to sales management.

Some Use-case scenarios

Use Case 1: CRM Systems

Scenario: Streamlining Sales Activities
Imagine you are a sales manager overseeing a team responsible for selling software solutions. By implementing a CRM system:

Centralized Customer Data: The CRM system allows your team to access a centralized database of customer information. When a sales representative interacts with a customer, they can quickly view the customer's history, preferences, and past purchases, enabling more personalized conversations.

Sales Pipeline Management: The CRM system helps manage the sales pipeline effectively. Through visual representations of the pipeline, you can identify bottlenecks, allocate resources efficiently, and forecast sales more accurately.

Automation of Routine Tasks: Routine tasks, such as sending follow-up emails or scheduling appointments, are automated within the CRM. This automation reduces manual workload, ensures consistency in communication, and allows the sales team to focus on building relationships.

Integration with Other Tools: The CRM seamlessly integrates with other tools, such as email platforms and project management software. This integration ensures a smooth flow of information across different systems, eliminating data silos and enhancing overall efficiency.

Use Case 2: Social Media and Sales
Scenario: Targeted Social Selling
In this scenario, you are a sales representative for a fashion brand. Leveraging social media:

Building an Online Presence: You establish a strong presence on platforms like Instagram and Pinterest, showcasing your brand's latest collections through visually appealing content. This online presence increases brand visibility and attracts a wider audience.

Targeted Social Selling: Using advanced search features on platforms like LinkedIn, you identify and connect with fashion influencers, stylists, and potential customers. Engaging with them directly allows for personalized interactions and the opportunity to showcase your brand's unique offerings.

Content Sharing and Thought Leadership: By consistently sharing fashion tips, trends, and behind-the-scenes content, you position yourself as a thought leader in the industry. This content not only engages your audience but also builds trust and credibility.

Social Listening: Monitoring social media for mentions of your brand and industry trends enables you to respond promptly to customer inquiries, address concerns, and stay ahead of changing preferences.

Use Case 3: Email Marketing Strategies

Scenario: Product Launch Campaign

Suppose you are a marketing manager planning the launch of a new tech gadget. Implementing email marketing strategies:

Segmentation: Your email list is segmented based on customer preferences, with categories such as tech enthusiasts, early adopters, and loyal customers. This segmentation allows for targeted messaging tailored to each group's interests.

Compelling Content: Craft an engaging email series that includes teaser videos, exclusive product insights, and limited-time pre-order offers. The content is designed to build anticipation, create a sense of exclusivity, and encourage recipients to take action.

Automation: Implementing email automation, you schedule a series of emails to be sent at specific intervals. Automation ensures that each subscriber receives a consistent and timed flow of information, maximizing engagement and conversion opportunities.

Analytics and Optimization: Using analytics tools, you track open rates, click-through rates, and conversion metrics. Insights from these metrics inform adjustments to the campaign strategy, allowing you to optimize email content for better performance.

Use Case 4: Using Data Analytics to Enhance Sales Performance

Scenario: Predictive Analytics for Lead Scoring

As a sales director for a software company, you implement predictive analytics to enhance lead scoring:

Predictive Analytics: By analyzing historical data, customer interactions, and purchase patterns, the predictive analytics model assigns scores to leads based on their likelihood to convert. This scoring system helps prioritize leads with the highest potential for conversion.

Customer Segmentation: The analytics model identifies distinct customer segments based on behavior, allowing for targeted marketing campaigns. For instance, you may create tailored promotions for customers who frequently engage with certain product features.

Sales Performance Metrics: Key performance indicators (KPIs) such as conversion rates, customer acquisition costs, and customer lifetime value are regularly monitored. These metrics provide insights into the effectiveness of sales strategies and guide decisions on resource allocation and strategic adjustments.

Data-Driven Decision Making: The sales team uses the insights from data analytics to refine marketing strategies, optimize the sales funnel, and allocate resources strategically. This data-driven approach enhances overall sales performance and customer satisfaction.

In each of these use cases, technology is seamlessly integrated into sales processes, demonstrating how CRM systems, social media strategies, email marketing, and data analytics contribute to enhanced efficiency, targeted communication, and informed decision-making in the sales domain. As you explore these technologies in your own sales efforts, consider how they can be tailored to meet the specific needs and objectives of your industry and target audience.

In the subsequent chapters, we will go through the art of closing deals, customer relationship management, and strategies for adapting to changing markets. As you integrate technology into your sales toolkit, remember that the goal is not just automation but enhancing the human touch in customer interactions and optimizing the overall sales process.

CHAPTER 5: CLOSING DEALS WITH IMPACTFUL TECHNIQUES

Closing a deal is the culmination of a well-executed sales process. In this chapter, we explore advanced techniques and strategies to master the art of closing deals effectively, leaving a lasting impact on both you and your customers.

5.1 Understanding Customer Buying Signals

Closing a deal begins with recognizing customer buying signals —indicators that the customer is ready to make a decision. These signals can be both verbal and non-verbal:

Verbal Signals:
- Expressed Intent: When a customer explicitly states their interest, such as "I'm ready to move forward" or "Let's proceed," it's a clear buying signal. In this case, take the opportunity to explore their motivations further. Ask questions like, "What specific aspects of our solution are most appealing to you?"

- Questions About Terms: When a customer seeks clarification on terms or conditions, provide a detailed explanation. Ensure they have a clear understanding of the terms and are comfortable moving forward. Inquiries about specific terms, pricing details, or contract conditions indicate a heightened interest in making a purchase.

Non-Verbal Signals:
- Body Language: Positive body language, such as nodding, leaning in, or maintaining eye contact, can signal agreement and readiness to move forward. Pay close attention to subtle cues like posture and gestures. A relaxed posture or affirmative nods indicate a positive disposition.
- Facial Expressions: A smile, relaxed facial features, or a focused expression may indicate a positive inclination towards closing the deal. If you notice positive facial expressions, use it as an opportunity to confirm their understanding of the value proposition. For example, "It seems like you resonate with the features we've discussed. Is that correct?"

5.2 Effective Trial Closes

Trial closes involve testing the waters to assess the customer's readiness to commit. These can be exploratory questions or statements that gauge their level of interest:

- Questioning Commitment: "How does this solution align with your needs?" or "Can you envision incorporating this into your workflow?" Pay attention to the customer's responses. If they express alignment with their needs, delve deeper into specific pain points to reinforce the value proposition.

- Proposal Recap: After summarizing key benefits, seek confirmation: "Based on our discussion, it appears our solution addresses your challenges. Are there any specific aspects you'd like to explore further?"

5.3 Overcoming Last-Minute Objections

In the final stages, objections may resurface. Address them with confidence:

- **Reiteration of Value**: Remind the customer of the unique value proposition and how your product or service meets their specific needs. Emphasize customization if applicable.

- **Case Studies/Testimonials**: Share relevant success stories or testimonials to alleviate concerns and build confidence in your offering.
This provides tangible proof of successful outcomes.

5.4 Closing Techniques

Mastering different closing techniques allows you to adapt to various situations. Some proven techniques include:

- **The Assumptive Close**: Assuming the close by using language that implies the deal is happening. For example, "When would you like delivery?" instead of "Would you like to proceed?"
NOTE: Before using this technique, ensure that the customer has given positive signals. For instance, if they've discussed implementation timeline, assume their commitment with a question like, "Shall we proceed with the agreed timeline?"

- **The Choice Close**: Presenting the customer with choices to guide their decision-making, such as "Would you prefer option A or option B?"
Tailor the choices based on the customer's preferences and needs. Offer options that align closely with their priorities.

- **The Urgency Close**: Creating a sense of urgency by highlighting limited-time offers or exclusive deals. "This special promotion ends this week—would you like to take advantage of it?" Clearly communicate the limited-time nature of the offer.

5.5 Negotiation Strategies for Win-Win Outcomes

Negotiation is a delicate balance. Aim for mutually beneficial outcomes:

- **Identify Priorities**: Understand the customer's priorities to negotiate effectively. Focus on aspects that matter most to them. Indepth Discussion: Engage in detailed discussions to uncover the customer's primary objectives. This can involve exploring their business goals, budget constraints, and specific requirements.

- **Give-and-Take**: Be willing to make concessions but ensure that you receive value in return. Establishing a fair exchange contributes to a positive negotiation process. Ensure that both parties feel they are receiving fair value.

5.6 Post-Close Follow-Up

Closing the deal is not the end; it's the beginning of a long-term relationship. Post-close follow-up steps include:

- **Express Gratitude**: Thank the customer for their trust and business. Customize your thank-you message based on the specifics of the deal. Express appreciation for their trust and highlight your excitement about the collaboration.

- **Onboarding Support**: Provide assistance with the onboarding process, ensuring a smooth transition. Anticipate potential challenges during onboarding and offer proactive assistance. This demonstrates your commitment to a smooth transition.

- **Ask for Feedback**: Seek feedback on the sales process and the product/service, emphasizing your commitment to continuous improvement. Phrase your feedback request in a way that encourages open communication. For example, "We value your input. Is there anything you believe we could improve in our sales process or product/service delivery?"

Certainly! Let's add more depth to Chapter 5 by exploring additional elements and nuances in closing deals with impactful techniques.

5.7 Handling Objections with Empathy

Handling objections empathetically is crucial in the closing stage. It involves not just addressing concerns but demonstrating genuine understanding and concern for the customer's perspective.

- Active Listening:

- **Empathetic Responses**: When addressing objections, rephrase the customer's concerns to show that you've heard and understood. Respond with empathy, acknowledging their perspective before presenting a solution.

- Alternative Solutions:

- **Collaborative Problem-Solving**: Instead of dismissing objections, work collaboratively with the customer to find alternative solutions. This approach reinforces a sense of partnership and commitment to their satisfaction.

5.8 Creating a Sense of Ownership

Encouraging customers to feel a sense of ownership in the decision-making process can significantly impact deal closure.

- Choice Empowerment:

- **Empowering Questions**: Pose questions that empower the customer to express ownership, such as "How do you envision implementing this solution within your team?" This fosters a sense of control and commitment.

- Customization Options:

- **Tailoring Solutions**: Allow customers to customize certain aspects of the deal, making it uniquely theirs. This customization enhances their sense of ownership and investment in the partnership.

5.9 Leveraging Social Proof

Social proof involves using evidence of others' positive experiences to influence the decision-making process.

- Case Studies and Testimonials:
  - **Strategic Placement:** Strategically incorporate relevant case studies and testimonials into your closing discussions. Highlighting similar successful partnerships creates a positive influence on the customer's decision.

- Peer References:
  - **Introduce Peer Success Stories:** If applicable, share success stories of companies similar to the customer's industry. Knowing that their peers have benefited from your solution can instill confidence.

5.10 Adapting to Decision-Making Styles

Understanding and adapting to different decision-making styles ensures that your approach resonates with diverse customers.

- Analytical Decision Makers:
  - **Data-Driven Insights:** Provide detailed data, analytics, and case studies to cater to the analytical mindset. Address their need for factual information to support the decision.

- Emotional Decision Makers:
  - **Emotional Connection:** Appeal to the emotional aspects of the decision. Highlight how the partnership will positively impact the team, workplace culture, or individual achievements.

5.11 Reinforcing Value Proposition

Reinforcing the value proposition throughout the closing process solidifies the customer's understanding of the benefits they will gain.

Value Recap:

- **Summarize Benefits**: Periodically recap the key benefits of your solution throughout the negotiation and closing stages. This reinforces the value and reminds the customer of the positive impact on their business.

Visual Aids:

-**Infographics or Visuals**: Utilize visual aids to represent the value proposition graphically. Visuals can make a lasting impression and enhance the customer's comprehension of the benefits.

5.12 Handling Post-Close Concerns

Even after the deal is closed, addressing any lingering concerns or uncertainties is essential for maintaining a positive relationship.

- Post-Close Check-In:

- **Follow-Up Communication**: Shortly after closing the deal, initiate a follow-up to check if the customer has any post-close concerns. Reassure them of ongoing support and commitment.

- Additional Resources:

- **Offer Support Resources**: Provide additional resources, such as user guides or tutorials, to ensure the customer feels equipped to maximize the value of the solution.

5.13 Ethical Considerations in Closing

Maintaining ethical standards in the closing process is fundamental for long-term customer relationships.

- Transparent Communication:

-**Honesty About Limitations**: Clearly communicate any limitations or potential challenges associated with your product or service. Transparency builds trust and prevents post-close disappointments.

- Avoiding Manipulation:

- **Genuine Intentions**: Ensure that your closing techniques focus on genuine customer needs rather than manipulating emotions or using high-pressure tactics. Ethical practices contribute to sustainable partnerships.

By incorporating these elements you not only enhance your understanding of closing techniques but also gain insights into the ethical considerations, adaptability to decision-making styles, and strategies for post-close success. Effective deal closure goes beyond the transaction; it establishes the foundation for a lasting and fruitful customer relationship.

Applying Techniques in Real-Life Scenarios

Consider applying these techniques in scenarios specific to your industry:

- **Technology Sales:** Emphasize the scalability, integration capabilities, and ongoing support of your technology solution and discuss how it aligns with the customer's long-term growth plans. Use trial closes to gauge their willingness to scale as needed.

- **Consulting Services:** Showcase the immediate and long-term impact of consulting services on the client's business goals.

- **E-commerce:** Leverage urgency in limited-time promotions and offer personalized product recommendations based on customer preferences. You may also use data analytics to offer personalized product recommendations. Use the urgency close for limited-time promotions, and trial closes to gauge their interest in specific product features.

As you master the art of closing deals, remember that

each customer interaction is unique. Continuously refine your approach, stay attuned to customer needs, and be adaptable in your closing techniques. Closing deals is not just about transactions; it's about creating value, building relationships, and fostering customer loyalty.

CHAPTER 6: CUSTOMER RELATIONSHIP MANAGEMENT STRATEGIES FOR LONG-TERM SUCCESS

Building and nurturing customer relationships is the cornerstone of sustained success in sales. In this chapter, we explore comprehensive Customer Relationship Management (CRM) strategies aimed at fostering long-term partnerships, customer loyalty, and advocacy.

6.1 The Role of CRM in Relationship Building

Understanding CRM Beyond Software:
- **Holistic Approach**: CRM is not just a software tool; it's a holistic approach to managing interactions and relationships with customers. It encompasses people, processes, and technology working in tandem.

Building a Customer-Centric Culture:
- **Organizational Alignment**: Ensure that every department

in your organization is aligned with a customer-centric culture. From sales and marketing to customer support, everyone plays a role in building and maintaining relationships.

6.2 Leveraging Data for Personalization

Customer Data Utilization:
- Data-Driven Insights: Use customer data to gain insights into preferences, behaviors, and engagement patterns. This information is invaluable for tailoring your interactions and offers to meet individual needs.

Personalized Communication:
- Segmentation and Targeting: Segment your customer base based on demographics, purchase history, or engagement levels. Craft personalized messages and offers to make customers feel seen and valued.

6.3 Proactive Customer Support and Engagement

Anticipating Customer Needs:
- Proactive Outreach: Anticipate customer needs by proactively reaching out with relevant information, updates, or resources. This demonstrates your commitment to their success.

Continuous Engagement:
- Feedback Loops: Establish feedback loops to consistently gather insights from customers. Act on this feedback to enhance your products, services, and overall customer experience.

6.4 Customer Retention Strategies

Loyalty Programs:
-Tailored Incentives: Implement loyalty programs with personalized incentives. Offer exclusive discounts, early access to new features, or special promotions to reward and retain loyal customers.

Relationship Check-Ins:
-Regular Touchpoints: Schedule periodic check-ins with key customers. Discuss their evolving needs, business goals, and how your solutions can continue to add value.

6.5 Managing Customer Expectations

Transparent Communication:
- Setting Realistic Expectations: From the initial sales pitch to ongoing interactions, be transparent about what customers can expect. Avoid overpromising and underdelivering.

Clear SLAs (Service Level Agreements):
- Agreed-upon Standards: Establish clear SLAs for your products or services. Ensure that both parties are aligned on expectations regarding delivery times, support response times, and any other critical parameters.

6.6 Recovering from Service Failures

Proactive Issue Resolution:
- Timely Communication: In the event of a service failure, communicate promptly with affected customers. Apologize sincerely, share your plan for resolution, and offer compensations if applicable.

Learning from Failures:
- Continuous Improvement: Use service failures as learning opportunities. Analyze root causes, implement corrective actions, and communicate the steps taken to prevent similar issues in the future.

6.7 Cross-Selling and Upselling Strategies

Strategic Recommendations:
-   Data-Driven   Suggestions: Utilize   CRM   data   to

make strategic cross-selling or upselling recommendations. Recommend products or services that align with the customer's needs and enhance their overall experience.

Educational Content:
- **Informative Resources:** Provide educational content on how additional offerings complement their current solutions. Demonstrating the added value encourages customers to explore expanded services.

6.8 Customer Advocacy Programs

Turning Customers into Advocates:
- **Identification of Advocates:** Identify satisfied customers who are likely to become advocates. These individuals can play a pivotal role in promoting your brand through testimonials, referrals, or case studies.

Recognition and Incentives:
- **Acknowledgment and Rewards:** Recognize and reward customer advocates for their efforts. This can include public acknowledgment, exclusive perks, or even participation in beta programs.

6.9 Measuring Customer Satisfaction and Loyalty

Key Metrics:
- **Net Promoter Score (NPS):** Implement metrics like NPS to measure overall customer satisfaction and likelihood to recommend your products or services to others.

Customer Feedback Surveys:
- **Regular Feedback Collection:** Conduct regular surveys to gather detailed feedback on specific aspects of your products, services, and customer interactions. Use this information to make targeted improvements.

6.10 Technology Integration for Seamless CRM

Unified Platforms:
- Integrated Systems: Ensure that your CRM system is seamlessly integrated with other business tools such as marketing automation, helpdesk software, and e-commerce platforms. This integration streamlines processes and enhances overall efficiency.

AI and Automation:
- Smart Automation: Leverage artificial intelligence (AI) for smart automation within your CRM. Automate routine tasks, analyze data for insights, and use AI-driven chatbots to enhance customer support.

6.11 Cultivating Long-Term Partnerships

Relationship Building Mindset:
- Long-Term Perspective: Approach every interaction with the mindset of building a long-term partnership rather than focusing solely on immediate transactions.

Account Management Teams:
- Dedicated Support: Assign account management teams to key clients. These teams serve as dedicated points of contact, fostering stronger relationships and a deeper understanding of customer needs.

6.12 Ethical Considerations in CRM

Privacy and Data Security:
- Stringent Security Measures: Implement robust privacy and data security measures. Customers should trust that their data is handled with the utmost care and used responsibly.

Transparency in Decision-Making:
- **Open Communication:** Be transparent about how customer data is used and the purposes behind specific CRM functionalities. Educate customers on how their information contributes to a personalized and improved experience.

By implementing these CRM strategies, you lay the foundation for enduring relationships with your customers. Remember, successful CRM is not just about managing data; it's about understanding, anticipating, and exceeding customer expectations at every stage of their journey with your brand.

CHAPTER 7: ADAPTING TO CHANGING MARKETS AND INDUSTRY TRENDS

The business landscape is dynamic, with markets and industries constantly evolving. In this chapter, we explore strategies to effectively adapt to changing market conditions and stay ahead of industry trends.

7.1 Continuous Market Analysis

Trend Monitoring:
- **Stay Informed:** Regularly monitor industry publications, market reports, and relevant news sources to stay abreast of emerging trends. Being well-informed allows you to proactively adjust your strategies.

Competitor Analysis:
- **Benchmarking:** Conduct regular competitor analyses to understand their strategies, strengths, and weaknesses. Identify areas where you can differentiate and capitalize on market gaps.

7.2 Agility in Product Development

Rapid Prototyping:
- **Agile Development:** Implement agile methodologies in product development. Use rapid prototyping to bring products to market quickly, allowing for timely adjustments based on customer feedback and market dynamics.

Beta Testing:
- **Customer Input:** Engage customers in beta testing phases to gather real-world feedback. Their insights can be invaluable in refining your product before a full-scale launch.

7.3 Flexibility in Marketing Strategies

Omni-Channel Marketing:
- **Diversify Channels:** Embrace an omni-channel marketing approach. Explore various channels, including social media, content marketing, and influencer partnerships, to reach diverse audience segments.

Data-Driven Campaigns:
- **Analytical Insights:** Use data analytics to evaluate the performance of marketing campaigns. Adjust strategies based on analytics to optimize for the channels and messaging that resonate most with your audience.

7.4 Embracing Technology Innovations

Early Adoption:
- **Technology Assessment:** Regularly assess emerging technologies relevant to your industry. Embrace innovations that align with your business goals, enhancing efficiency and providing a competitive edge.

AI and Machine Learning:
- **Predictive Analytics:** Leverage AI and machine learning for

predictive analytics. These technologies can analyze vast datasets, helping you forecast trends, identify opportunities, and make informed decisions.

7.5 Strategic Partnerships and Collaborations

Industry Alliances:
- **Collaborative Ventures:** Form strategic partnerships with other businesses in your industry. Collaborative ventures can lead to shared resources, knowledge exchange, and mutually beneficial projects.

Joint Marketing Efforts:
- **Coordinated Campaigns:** Explore joint marketing efforts with strategic partners. Coordinated campaigns can amplify your reach and introduce your brand to new audiences.

7.6 Talent Development and Training

Continuous Learning:
- **Employee Training Programs:** Invest in ongoing training programs for your team. Equip them with the skills needed to adapt to new technologies and industry trends.

Cross-Functional Teams:
- **Collaborative Skillsets:** Foster cross-functional collaboration within your organization. Teams with diverse skill sets can collectively address challenges and devise innovative solutions.

7.7 Customer Feedback and Market Surveys

Regular Feedback Collection:
- **Customer Surveys:** Conduct regular surveys to gather feedback on your products, services, and overall customer experience. Use this data to identify areas for improvement and

align your offerings with customer expectations.

Market Research:
- **Targeted Research Initiatives:** Initiate targeted market research initiatives to gain deeper insights into customer needs, preferences, and behaviors. Research findings can inform strategic decisions.

7.8 Crisis Preparedness and Risk Management

Scenario Planning:
- **Risk Assessments:** Conduct regular risk assessments to identify potential threats to your business. Develop contingency plans and scenario-based strategies to navigate unforeseen challenges.

Crisis Communication:
- **Transparent Communication:** In times of crisis, communicate transparently with your customers. Address concerns proactively, share your mitigation strategies, and reassure them of your commitment to their well-being.

7.9 Regulatory Compliance

Compliance Audits:
- **Regular Audits:** Stay vigilant about regulatory changes impacting your industry. Conduct regular compliance audits to ensure your business practices align with evolving legal requirements.

Legal Counsel:
- **Legal Advisory Support:** Establish relationships with legal experts or firms specializing in your industry. Seek their counsel to stay ahead of regulatory changes and ensure your business

remains compliant.

7.10 Sustainability Practices

Environmental and Social Responsibility:
- **Ethical Practices:** Embrace sustainability practices that align with environmental and social responsibility. Consumers increasingly value businesses committed to ethical and sustainable operations.

Green Innovation:
- **Eco-Friendly Initiatives:** Innovate with eco-friendly products or processes. Green initiatives not only contribute to sustainability but also resonate with a growing segment of environmentally conscious consumers.

7.11 Cultural Sensitivity and Globalization

Cultural Competence:
- **Diversity Training:** Invest in diversity and cultural competence training for your team. Understanding and respecting diverse cultures is crucial in a globalized market.

Localization Strategies:
- **Tailored Offerings:** Implement localization strategies in your products and marketing. Tailor offerings to specific cultural nuances and preferences, ensuring relevance in diverse markets.

7.12 Building Resilience

Scenario Planning:
- **Resilience Frameworks:** Develop resilience frameworks that include scenario planning, risk assessments, and crisis management strategies. Being resilient enables your business to weather challenges and emerge stronger.

Adaptive Leadership:
- **Adaptive Leadership Skills:** Cultivate adaptive leadership skills within your organization. Leaders who can navigate change with agility inspire resilience and innovation among their teams.

In a rapidly evolving business landscape, adaptability is the key to sustained success. By embracing change, leveraging emerging technologies, and cultivating a culture of continuous learning, your business can not only survive but thrive in dynamic markets and shifting industry trends.

This chapter underscores the critical importance of adaptability in navigating the ever-evolving business landscape. As markets and industries undergo constant change, businesses must proactively embrace strategies that allow them to stay ahead of trends, respond to challenges, and foster long-term success.

By adopting a mindset of continuous market analysis, businesses can remain well-informed about emerging trends and dynamically adjust their strategies. This involves not only monitoring industry publications but also conducting competitor analyses to identify opportunities for differentiation.

Agility in product development is another key facet, emphasizing the importance of rapid prototyping and customer engagement through beta testing. This allows businesses to bring products to market swiftly, incorporating valuable feedback and ensuring relevance.

Flexibility in marketing strategies, including an omni-channel approach and data-driven campaigns, enables businesses to reach diverse audiences effectively. Moreover, embracing technological innovations, such as AI and machine learning, positions organizations to harness predictive analytics and gain a competitive edge.

Strategic partnerships and collaborations provide avenues for shared resources, knowledge exchange, and expanded market reach. Investing in talent development and training ensures that teams are equipped with the skills needed to adapt to new technologies and industry trends.

Customer feedback and market surveys play a pivotal role in staying attuned to evolving customer needs. Additionally, crisis preparedness, risk management, regulatory compliance, sustainability practices, and cultural sensitivity contribute to building resilience in the face of challenges.

In conclusion, businesses that prioritize adaptability, strategic foresight, and a commitment to continuous improvement are better positioned to thrive amid the dynamic nature of modern markets. The ability to anticipate change, pivot when necessary, and capitalize on emerging opportunities is the cornerstone of sustained success in an ever-changing business landscape.

THE FINAL CHAPTER: SUSTAINING EXCELLENCE AND FOSTERING INNOVATION

Sustaining excellence in sales requires a commitment to ongoing innovation and a mindset that embraces change. In this chapter, we explore strategies to foster innovation within your sales organization, ensuring a dynamic and forward-thinking approach to business.

8.1 Cultivating a Culture of Innovation

Leadership Support:
- **Encouraging Creativity:** Leaders play a pivotal role in fostering innovation. Encourage a culture where team members feel empowered to voice ideas, take calculated risks, and explore creative solutions.

Recognition for Innovative Contributions:
- **Acknowledging Innovation:** Implement systems that recognize and reward innovative contributions. This can include regular awards, public acknowledgment, or opportunities for professional development.

8.2 Continuous Learning and Professional Development

Investment in Training Programs:
- **Skill Enhancement:** Invest in ongoing training programs to enhance the skills of your sales team. Equip them with the latest industry knowledge, technological advancements, and sales techniques.

Cross-Functional Collaboration:
- **Learning from Other Departments:** Foster collaboration with other departments, allowing team members to learn from diverse perspectives. This cross-functional approach can spark new ideas and approaches.

8.3 Technology Integration for Efficiency

Advanced CRM Systems:
- **AI and Automation Integration:** Continuously explore advancements in CRM systems. Integrate AI and automation tools to streamline processes, analyze customer data more efficiently, and enhance overall productivity.

Sales Enablement Platforms:
- **Empowering Sales Teams:** Implement sales enablement platforms that provide centralized access to training materials, product information, and sales collateral. This ensures that your sales team is well-equipped to deliver exceptional value.

8.4 Agile Sales Strategies

Iterative Approach:
- **Adaptable Sales Plans:** Embrace an iterative approach to sales strategies. Regularly review and adjust plans based on performance metrics, market changes, and customer feedback.

Experimentation and A/B Testing:
- **Data-Driven Decision Making**: Encourage experimentation through A/B testing in sales campaigns. Analyze the results to make data-driven decisions and refine your approach for optimal outcomes.

8.5 Customer-Centric Innovation

Co-Creation with Customers:
- **Customer Feedback Forums**: Establish channels for customer feedback and suggestions. Actively involve customers in the co-creation process, ensuring that your products and services align closely with their evolving needs.

Beta Testing and Pilot Programs:
- **Early Customer Adoption**: Prioritize beta testing and pilot programs where customers can experience new features or offerings before full-scale implementation. Their insights provide valuable input for improvements.

8.6 Employee Empowerment

Autonomy and Decision-Making Authority:
- **Empowering Teams**: Grant teams the autonomy to make decisions within their areas of expertise. Empowered teams are more likely to generate innovative solutions and take ownership of their projects.

Intrapreneurship Programs:
- **Encouraging Intrapreneurship**: Implement intrapreneurship programs that allow employees to explore entrepreneurial ideas within the organization. This stimulates a culture of innovation from within.

8.7 Metrics for Innovation Assessment

Innovation Key Performance Indicators (KPIs):
- **Establishing KPIs:** Develop specific KPIs to measure innovation within your sales organization. These can include the number of implemented ideas, improvements in customer satisfaction, and the success rate of innovative projects.

Continuous Improvement Feedback:
- **Feedback Mechanisms:** Create mechanisms for continuous improvement feedback. Regularly solicit input from team members, customers, and stakeholders to refine and optimize your innovative strategies.

8.8 Embracing Change and Risk

Risk-Taking Culture:
- **Positive Attitude Toward Risk:** Cultivate a culture where calculated risks are embraced. Encourage team members to step outside their comfort zones, knowing that innovation often involves a degree of uncertainty.

Learning from Setbacks:
- **Debriefing and Analysis:** When innovations do not go as planned, conduct thorough debriefings and analyses. Extract lessons from setbacks to inform future endeavors and reinforce a culture of continuous improvement.

8.9 Future-Forward Vision

Trend Anticipation:
- **Scanning the Horizon:** Develop a forward-looking mindset by constantly scanning the business landscape for emerging trends. Anticipate shifts in customer behaviors, technological advancements, and market dynamics.

Scenario Planning for Future Challenges:
- **Strategic Preparedness:** Engage in scenario planning to

anticipate and prepare for future challenges. Develop strategic initiatives that position your sales organization to thrive amid evolving circumstances.

8.10 Celebrating Innovation Milestones

Milestone Recognition:
- **Celebrating Achievements:** Celebrate innovation milestones within your sales organization. Whether it's the successful launch of a new product or the implementation of a groundbreaking strategy, recognition fosters a culture of achievement.

Knowledge Sharing:
- **Internal Knowledge-Sharing Platforms:** Create internal platforms where innovative ideas and success stories are shared. This not only inspires others but also promotes a collaborative atmosphere.

8.11 Sustainability in Innovation

Long-Term Impact Assessment:
- **Environmental and Social Considerations:** Integrate sustainability into your innovation initiatives. Assess the long-term impact of new products or strategies on environmental and social factors.

Responsible Innovation Practices:
- **Ethical and Inclusive Innovation:** Ensure that innovation practices are guided by ethical considerations and inclusivity. Responsible innovation practices contribute to positive brand perception.

8.12 Legacy Building and Succession Planning

Knowledge Transfer:
- **Mentorship Programs:** Establish mentorship programs

to facilitate knowledge transfer. Seasoned team members can mentor newer ones, ensuring that institutional knowledge and innovative thinking are passed down.

Succession Planning for Leadership:

- **Identifying Future Leaders:** Implement succession planning strategies to identify and groom future leaders within your sales organization. This ensures a seamless transition and the continuity of innovative practices.

In conclusion, sustaining excellence in sales is not just about meeting current benchmarks but also about fostering a culture of innovation that adapts to change and anticipates the future. By cultivating a mindset of continuous improvement, empowering teams, and embracing the dynamic nature of the business landscape, your sales organization can thrive in the face of evolving challenges and opportunities.

CONCLUSION

In concluding this comprehensive guide on sales, we have explored the fundamental principles, advanced strategies, and forward-thinking approaches that contribute to a successful and sustainable sales journey. Let's summarize the key takeaways from each chapter:

Chapter 1: Introduction to Sales Excellence
- Defined the essence of sales and its impact on business success.
- Emphasized the role of customer-centricity in building lasting relationships.

Chapter 2: Understanding the Fundamentals of Sales
- Explored the definition and importance of sales.
- Provided a step-by-step overview of the sales process.
- Distinguished between B2B and B2C sales.
- Highlighted the significance of emotional intelligence in sales.

Chapter 3: Building a Strong Sales Foundation
- Discussed the importance of developing a sales mindset.
- Introduced the concept of SMART sales goals.
- Emphasized the need to know your product inside out.
- Addressed the significance of identifying your target audience.

Chapter 4: Effective Sales Techniques
- Explored essential communication and persuasion techniques.
- Provided insights into objection handling and relationship building.
- Highlighted the power of storytelling in sales.

Chapter 5: Advanced Closing Strategies

- Delved into understanding customer buying signals.
- Explored effective trial closes and overcoming objections.
- Introduced various closing techniques and negotiation strategies.
- Discussed post-close follow-up and customer feedback.

Chapter 6: Customer Relationship Management Strategies for Long-Term Success

- Explored the role of CRM in relationship building.
- Discussed leveraging data for personalization.
- Emphasized proactive customer support, loyalty programs, and managing customer expectations.
- Touched on recovery from service failures, cross-selling, upselling, and customer advocacy.

Chapter 7: Adapting to Changing Markets and Industry Trends

- Discussed continuous market analysis and agility in product development.
- Emphasized flexibility in marketing strategies and embracing technology innovations.
- Explored the importance of strategic partnerships, talent development, and customer feedback.
- Tackled crisis preparedness, regulatory compliance, sustainability, and cultural sensitivity.

Chapter 8: Sustaining Excellence and Fostering Innovation

- Explored cultivating a culture of innovation and continuous learning.
- Discussed technology integration, agile sales strategies, and customer-centric innovation.
- Emphasized employee empowerment, metrics for innovation assessment, and embracing change and risk.
- Touched on future-forward vision, celebrating innovation milestones, sustainability, and legacy building.

In essence, this guide aims to equip you with a holistic understanding of sales, from foundational principles to advanced strategies, and encourages a mindset of continuous improvement and innovation. Sustaining excellence in sales is a dynamic journey that involves adapting to change, fostering lasting relationships, and consistently striving for innovation.

As you embark on your sales endeavors, may the insights and strategies provided in this guide serve as a valuable companion on your path to achieving sales excellence. Best of luck in your sales endeavors, and may your journey be filled with growth, success, and enduring relationships with your valued customers.

Best Wishes
Saurabh Kumar

ACKNOWLEDGEMENT

Writing a book is a journey that involves the support and contribution of many individuals who play crucial roles in its creation. As I reflect on the completion of this guide on sales excellence, I am grateful for the encouragement, insights, and collaborative spirit of those who have been instrumental in bringing this project to fruition.

A special thanks to Aman for your unwavering support and constructive feedback. Your keen insights and dedication to the project have significantly enriched the final product.

I would like to express my gratitude to all the seniors and colleagues from Meritnation, Analytics Vidhya and ICRI, whose mentorship has been the fuel, without which this couldn't have been possible.

To the entire Analytics Vidhya team, thank you for fostering an environment that encourages innovation and excellence. Your commitment to maintain a healthy atmosphere has inspired the ethos of this guide.

I extend my appreciation to the numerous individuals who graciously shared their experiences and perspectives during interviews and discussions. Your real-world insights have brought authenticity and practicality to the concepts discussed.

Lastly, a heartfelt thank you to my friends and family for their unwavering support and understanding during the demanding phases of writing. Your encouragement fueled my determination to create a guide that is both informative and engaging.

I am sincerely grateful.

Warm regards,
Saurabh Kumar